A special wish

Martin Debattista

Print information available on the last page

Rev. date: 11/17/2018

To order additional copies of this book, contact:
Xlibris
1-888-795-4274
www.Xlibris.com
Orders@Xlibris.com

A special wish

Martin DeBattista

Illustrated by Al C. Cabagnot

For my son Ryan and my daughter Leanne:
Don't ever be afraid to dream. People
who dream can change the world.

I love you, Daddy

So excellent is Your love, oh Lord,
So wondrous are Your ways.

So precious are Your tears, oh God,
I live to give You praise.

In appreciation -

I wish to express sincere appreciation to Charlotte Buhmann and her son, Scott Buhmann, for editing, layout and assistance in the publishing process. Your guidance and support has been invaluable to me.

The first time I wished upon a star,

I didn't know what to say.

I looked up to the sky,

they seemed so far away.

1

I saw so many stars;

which one did I see first?

My stomach seemed so nervous,

I thought that it might burst!

So, I closed my eyes to make a wish,

and then I had a thought.

My wish had to be special,

not something made nor bought.

- - - - -

I thought for a minute about

other girls and boys.

Maybe they were wishing

for lots of colored toys.

But, maybe they were wishing
for a place to lay their head.
Their wish seemed so special,
so, I wished their wish instead.

Somehow, I felt better,

in a very special way.

I'll never see my wish come true,

but my wish was special anyway.

A Collection of Poems

Daddy

I love to walk in the sand
and get it stuck between my toes, and to roll down a hill
while the grass tickles my nose.

Walk around the block, or be an Olympic
star! Look up to the stars,
and dream of places afar.

But, what I like the most is when the world is still,
and your heart beats on my cheek,
and love is what I feel.

And, I know you feel it too because there's a smile
on your face. Your heart beat on my cheek
will always be my favorite place.

I love you both;
it's my favorite place too!

Dad

Help Me, I'm Cold

I am cold.

My body is shaking.

If I go to sleep, I am afraid I will not awake.

There is ice on my beard.

There is no sun.

I cannot stand up, walk. My stomach
is empty. My heart is frozen.
Tomorrow holds no promise, Hope.

If I had a wish, what would I wish for?

I would wish to be happy.

Good night.

Aided by His Mercy

A river running through me.
Turning water into dust.
The blood of our sweet Savior. Whose
knowledge we entrust.

My grace be with you always. For, you need not
fear the Lord. His mercy endures forever.
He gave to us His Word.

Be thankful for this minute. You hold it in your hand.
Just like an oyster forms a pearl
when it holds a grain of sand.

God's will works through each of us.
His will is always done. That's why He sent
among us Our Savior and His Son.

He taught us not to fear our God, but to
seek Him in our heart. Whatever point we
are in life, it's not too late to start.

So, be comforted in knowing you shall never stand alone. God's river of love keeps flowing like a river over stone.

Luck

I have many scars.

Silent, hidden, bright and strong
wonderment and uncertainty.

My body at times is weakened,
yet I will not allow my spirit.

I MUST move forward.

Yesterday is gone, tomorrow is a lifetime away.

Today, the silent calls of the wind
shall form a new horizon.

Tomorrow, I may be rich or poor, yet I will still be me.

If I live for today,
what have I gained?

I have gained a new yesterday.

Humble Heart

There once lived a man, and he still lives today.
He taught us of life and of things that we should say.
Our minds as they wander, our feet as they stray.
Our sisters we hurt, our brothers we betray.
Can we not learn a lesson that life is a true treasure?
Each day we complete should always be a pleasure!
For in our daily suffering, we nary stop and pray.
Let alone give thanks and praise for the glory of today.
This man he gave of himself in ways we never could.
And yet, we think of ourselves in ways we think we should.
The wonder of a sunset, the beauty of a flower,
Things we cannot understand, the awesome strength and power.
I give to you my love. I want to serve your will.
I know at times I may fail, yet you will love me still.
Then we will all be happy, for we know your love will please us.
Your love will resurrect us, we know your name is Jesus.

Printed in the United States
By Bookmasters